THE NATIONAL POETRY SERIES

The National Poetry Series was established in 1978 to ensure the publication of five poetry books annually through participating publishers. Publication is funded by the Lannan Foundation; the late James A. Michener and Edward J. Piszek through the Copernicus Society of America; Stephen Graham; International Institute of Modern Letters; Joyce & Seward Johnson Foundation; Juliet Lea Hillman Simonds Foundation; and the Tiny Tiger Foundation. This project is also supported in part by an award from the National Endowment for the Arts, which believes that a great nation deserves great art.

2005 COMPETITION WINNERS

STEVE GEHRKE
of Columbia, Missouri, *Michelangelo's Seizure*
Chosen by T. R. Hummer, published by University of Illinois Press

NADINE MEYER
of Columbia, Missouri, *The Anatomy Theater*
Chosen by John Koethe, published by HarperCollins

PATRICIA SMITH
of Tarrytown, New York, *Teahouse of the Almighty*
Chosen by Edward Sanders, published by Coffee House Press

S. A. STEPANEK
of West Chicago, Illinois, *Three, Breathing*
Chosen by Mary Ruefle, published by Wave Books

TRYFON TOLIDES
of Farmington, Connecticut, *An Almost Pure Empty Walking*
Chosen by Mary Karr, published by Penguin Books

NATIONAL
ENDOWMENT
FOR THE ARTS

THREE, BREATHING

THREE,

THE NATIONAL POETRY SERIES
SELECTED BY
MARY RUEFLE

S. A. STEPANEK

BREATHING

WAVE BOOKS

SEATTLE

NEW YORK

Published by Wave Books

www.wavepoetry.com

Wave Books titles are distributed to the trade
by Consortium Book Sales and Distribution
1045 Westgate Drive, St. Paul, Minnesota 55114

Library of Congress Cataloging-in-Publication Data
Stepanek, S. A., 1960–
Three, breathing / S. A. Stepanek.— 1st ed.
p. cm. — (The national poetry series)
ISBN 1-933517-13-1 (alk. paper) —
ISBN 1-933517-12-3 (trade pbk. : alk. paper)
I. Title: 3, breathing. II. Title. III. Series.
PS3619.T47655T47 2006
811'.6—dc22
2006000039

Excerpts from this book were
previously published in *The Iowa Review*.

Designed and composed by Quemadura
Printed in the United States of America

9 8 7 6 5 4 3 2 1

FIRST EDITION

TO GOD BE THE GLORY

THREE, BREATHING

I am ashamed before speech
on the margins
of dictionaries.

I am ashamed before speech
collapsing in
the general thesaurus.

I am ashamed before the Great between
becomings, holy palms of mirrors, holy
water harbors.

I am ashamed before the Great nonexit
stone which has flown from the palm now
crossing this river.

I am ashamed before the Great substantial
chair, my
love.

I am ashamed before the Great
unsubstantial chair larger than
visible light.

I am ashamed before the Great intrinsic
sacred
sounds, three.

I am ashamed before the Great extrinsic
folding over burlap
as if for the first time.

I am ashamed before the Great state
calling my name.

I am ashamed before the Great circumstance
falling from trees and roots
and falling from trees and roots.

I am ashamed before the Great relation
speaking
a blank stone, as if.

I am ashamed before the Great
unrelatedness, the center of trees and
cascading caves.

I am ashamed before the Great relation in
blood calling
morning by morning.

I am ashamed before the Great relation
marrying before,
thrice, before me.

I am ashamed before the Great correlation
of fathers on floors
for this I must know he lives.

I am ashamed before the Great identity
above before us
with the wrists of all doves.

I am ashamed before the
Great contrariety
with which I am clothed.

I am ashamed before the Great
difference of small
fish.

I am ashamed before the Great uniformity
of our mended
clothes.

I am ashamed before the Great
nonuniformity of
ours.

I am ashamed before the Great similarity
of gray lines between lines and taking
this forgiveness.

I am ashamed before the Great
dissimilarity of rock and flesh.

I am ashamed before the Great imitation of
returning.

I am ashamed before the Great nonimitation
of mind waking up and mind waking up.

I am ashamed before the Great copy
turning the mirror in a turn in the mirror
of a self above and a self.

I am ashamed before the Great
model of her pacing
as she erased clouds, I forgive her.

I am ashamed before the Great agreement of
clouds erasing themselves
because they are clothed.

I am ashamed before the Great disagreement
of hands from above
because I hear the breath above wires.

I am ashamed before the Great quantity of
his glyph of nothing,
mountains upon great mountains, mountains.

I am ashamed before the Great degree of
his shape and stillness.

I am ashamed before the Great equality of
his seed spilled around him,
for this we have all been forgiven.

I am ashamed before the Great mean between
what we call color
and the great white rope hauling us in.

I am ashamed before the Great compensation
following bloodstones following suns on
the grass and the coin of its wearing.

I am ashamed before the Great greatness
the signs are spreading, for
this I am wholly.

I am ashamed before the Great smallness of
the fertilizing machine
and willows to be pruned.

I am ashamed before the Great superiority
before I slept
past first effects, past that.

I am ashamed before the Great inferiority
of the call for the call, when the
notes slow and you hear them.

I am ashamed before the Great increase of
small seeds in beds
and bosom-bedding mountains.

I am ashamed before the Great
decrease of wondering and waiting
before being clothed from outside.

I am ashamed before the Great addition,
because we saw the right from the left
as the notes taught us to walk.

I am ashamed before the Great
adjunct and am cold and am gladly
as I am gladly heard, coming back.

I am ashamed before the Great subtraction
and sit in a red chair.

I am ashamed before the Great remainder in
the bell and the cup and
the one candle's highest harmonies.

I am ashamed before the Great mixture,
her reading the place of the clouds
she once saw on the garage floor.

I am ashamed before the Great simplicity
between the kitchen and garage.

I am ashamed before the Great complexity
as I run
through doors and past newspapers.

I am ashamed before the Great joining the
need for the turn and the knowing of
the need.

I am ashamed before the Great analysis of
the bed.

I am ashamed before the Great separation
of sheets and books
having left the house entitled here.

I am ashamed before the Great cohesion
passing things as we leave them
as spring unmoors us tomorrow.

I am ashamed before the Great noncohesion
between how kisses
from a little sister must bow before
(we must continue to seek the General).

I am ashamed before the Great combination
he rewrites on the floor,
third love letters, first hands we are.

I am ashamed before the Great
disintegration rewritten under trees
for ours is her port.

I am ashamed before the Great whole I
called.

I am ashamed before the Great
part
of the night lamp.

I am ashamed before the Great completeness
engraved there
of the delta where morning extinguishes.

I am ashamed before the Great incomplete
of my small bed
and your vast pastures, lay me down, O.

I am ashamed before the Great composition
of maps matching exactly.

I am ashamed before the Great order I lie
about.

I am ashamed before the Great arrangement
of eyes being beyond in the night.

I am ashamed before the Great disorder of
earth over we were a small bed of us
between ourselves.

I am ashamed before the Great
disarrangement of four balls in a box and
a back in a pew and the time returning.

I am ashamed before the Great precedence:
because of small notations
we slip off the edge and are—

I am ashamed before the Great sequence of
shame which makes the tea
and strokes the face.

I am ashamed before the Great precursor as
the keys reversed
are and will be, and were to come.

I am ashamed before the Great sequel to
the left and right halves of me, he
enclosed me above and before, amen.

I am ashamed before the
Great beginning, his right hand lays hold.

I am ashamed before the Great middle when
39 seconds scatter from the garage to the
kitchen to the garage to the kitchen.

I am ashamed before the Great end dividing
between from before from between from be-

I am ashamed before the Great continuity:
the grass efforts to the flower
the grass' great worlds before the world—

I am ashamed before the Great
discontinuity edging the cedars
before the world was.

I am ashamed before the Great
accompaniment of cracks falling in air
toward Chebar.

I am ashamed before the Great
assemblage love which assembles my
arms as rivers: I lay them down and I in
them.

I am ashamed before the Great dispersion
sitting in pews
and coming toward my burlap and I am with
them.

I am ashamed before the Great inclusion
which rests as he sleeps, this heart
heading west and east, running, re-
turning.

I am ashamed before the Great exclusion of
small animals, small
fish, smaller fish just arriving.

I am ashamed before the Great extraneous
way
between states, keeping us in cars.

I am ashamed before the Great generality
after this.

I am ashamed before the Great
particularity of the door and the wind as
I see him.

I am ashamed before the Great speciality
becoming heard,
despite itself.

I am ashamed before the Great conformity
witnessing night returning to the delta,
becoming light, for this I say amen amen

I am ashamed before the Great
nonconformity on the floor above him above
which I say nevermore and invite myself.

I am ashamed before the Great normality as
one speaks to stone.

I am ashamed before the Great abnormality
higher than tree-thoughts
and needing no music to climb.

I am ashamed before the Great number
of you, sideways
sunning themselves in your snow mountain.

I am ashamed before the Great numeration
not according to what we know
which calls those things which be not.

I am ashamed before the Great
list at the bottom of the stairs
which called my name upon it.

I am ashamed before the Great unity which
is the forest within a clearing within the
clear.

I am ashamed before the Great duality
between the center of wood
and the washing by water.

I am ashamed before the Great duplication
larger than visible speech
and the eyes which have eyes to see.

I am ashamed before the Great bisection of
words in light
as the seven flock to the first morning.

I am ashamed before the Great three
breathing
and the woman who waits by the well.

I am ashamed before the Great delta winds
writing a face for the sky
beginning to walk.

I am ashamed before the Great trisection
of grass the color of roses
grasses the color of roses
great, great harvests, risen snows.

I am ashamed before the Great four shapes
of sound
which call fields, moon, color, grasses.

I am ashamed before the Great
quadruplication of north twice over
calling itself beloved.

I am ashamed before the Great
quadrisection of wood
spinning in light.

I am ashamed before the Great
holy emptiness
like a ball in an empty tomb.

I am ashamed before the Great plurality in
other directions
spinning in my palms.

I am ashamed before the Great numerous
spilling green
as we walk to St. Peter's this morning.

I am ashamed before the Great fewness
in the end,
so gladly found.

I am ashamed of the Great repetition
I am ashamed before the Great repetition
so gladly found, with its palms out.

I am ashamed before the Great
infinity
which must be coming and is this morning.

I am ashamed before
the knowing of the Great
time of the call.

I am ashamed before the Great timelessness
rising in me this morning
of great blankets and birth.

I am ashamed before the Great period
of the forgiven garage
where we first found the father.

I am ashamed before the Great
spelling of seeds
in green grasses.

I am ashamed before
the setting sun—for we have done so
little today—the ends now beginning.

And as I am ashamed before returning
all errors of forgetfulness
seen for a top moment from the top half.

And I am ashamed before the interim;
lovely ark to the edges of vision,
guiding me with his eye.

I am ashamed before all durability
from the back pages forward,
and I kneel before the Great spin.

I am ashamed before the Great transience
of green wheels
in grass, roses of grasses and roses.

I am ashamed before the
Great perpetual wheel I read
in the general rising.

I am ashamed before the Great, great
instant
in the arc of the interior palm.

I am ashamed before the Great I am ashamed
before the measurement of time as we
collapse between its arms.

I am ashamed before the Great I am
anachronism in the rock before the rock
before the letter of the before.

I am ashamed before the Great prior
reaching toward, bursting its wind
skins within me.

I am ashamed before the Great
posteriority. And for you I am gladly
found.

I am ashamed before the Great simultaneous
wind, oh—
lay your hand at port.

I am ashamed before the Great past.
I am ashamed before this great invasion.
And the line between concrete and skin
beside all wells.

I am ashamed before the Great present.
For this, still, yet, indeed we are in the
of and the as and the great white sheet of
our deserts.

I am ashamed before the Great future you
who moor me with green sequels,
flocks of grasses.

I am ashamed before the Great newness of
ten apples and spoons safe in drawers.

I am ashamed before the Great ancient
always-coming, always-going.

I am ashamed before the Great young
bow bending white willows, the first form
of present forgiveness.

I am ashamed before the Great youngster
unmooring spring after
winter turns back.

I am ashamed before the Great age
of the dead.

I am ashamed before the Great old mother I
thought awake.

I am ashamed before the Great season when
I thought I was on earth.

I am ashamed before the Great timeliness
how high do I lift off the page how far
left do I go how long do I

am ashamed before the Great untimeliness
of apples in the refrigerator is he cold
as I am cold.

I am ashamed before the Great earliness in
the midst of the kitchen.

I am ashamed before the Great lateness in
the door to the garage and darkness.

I am ashamed before the Great morning
speaking to darkness from darkness and
doors.

I am ashamed before the Great evening
leading me in although I am afraid.

I am ashamed before the Great frequency
going back and going to the back of the
body am I under him under me are we.

I am ashamed before the Great infrequency
of the way
in which we love.

I am ashamed before the Great regularity
of recurrence as a wound between beds.

I am ashamed before the Great irregularity
of recurrence as a slap and erasure as
never final and now is.

I am ashamed before the Great change
is kindness and kind:
it is late.

I am ashamed before the Great permanence
of turns in silk scarf drawers or deserts.

I am ashamed before the Great
changeableness of our small hands on
tables.

I am ashamed before the Great stability of
color when crossing the line: this is the first rule filling the
box.

I am ashamed before the Great continuance
of the cars following streets.

I am ashamed before the Great cessation of
planes in air and wooden spoons in drawers
whittled away my old desert my old garage.

I am ashamed before the Great conversion
it was yellow within me it was yellow next
to me it was yellow around me desert sky
no-desert sky

I am ashamed before the Great reversion of
the line between the blue and the green
and the great wheels over lawns.

I am ashamed before the Great revolution
under old mounds
in the desert airs.

I am ashamed before the Great evolution of
one note following.

I am ashamed before the Great substitution
of yellow cones turning end to end front
to future.

I am ashamed before the Great interchange
among children in trees
falling from your branch.

I am ashamed before the Great event of
leaves
rising and roads following cars.

I am ashamed before the Great imminence
following breath and a circular stair.

I am ashamed before the Great cause, the
kitchen, the apples, the lawn, the father,
the need for the father and the knowing of
the need.

I am ashamed before the Great effect
opening to the right page, erasing
the erasing of erasing itself.

And I am ashamed before the Great
attribution of small things with many
doubles, which, in fact, is this.

I am ashamed before the Great chance
always already calling from the stair we
are holding too tightly.

I am ashamed before the Great potency of
misdirection and velocity rearriving, and
for this I am afraid.

I am ashamed before the Great Impotence
who would be reading the pool or the river
or the flesh or the sky or the branch.

I am ashamed before the Great Strength of
both ends bare and all four tires: of
this I am sorely afraid.

I am ashamed before the Great Weaker
Weaning away from this strength and the
need for the knowing of the known and.

I am ashamed before the Great Energy
wingtips and wheels folded in chairs: I
am amazed to be lame.

I am ashamed before the Great Violence of
pilots dreaming of Chuang Tzu
or the wild bush
just before
catching on fire.

I am ashamed before the Great moderation
there were ten he was breathing at the
kitchen table.

I am ashamed before the Great operation he
was reading the paper and drinking coffee
and the coffee pot was about to take off.

I am ashamed before the Great productive
pavilion and house myself
in its farthest quarter.

I am ashamed before the Great unproductive
of white boys in Keokuk
and count myself and my husbands.

I am ashamed before the Great
Birth,
Shadows, holy desert palms.

I am ashamed before the Great
product erasing itself as it moves through
clouds

I am ashamed before the Great Procreation,
the old, old story.
Did you know I was flying there?

I am ashamed before the Great Ancestry.
I am ashamed before this great hovering
above not wanting to come to the table.

I am ashamed before the Posterity of the
marriage
and invite myself because I am found.

I am ashamed before the Great Influence
that burst the skin that drank the wine
that walked in the deserts flying above

I am ashamed before the Great Absence and
cracks spilling over ceilings and running
up wooden walls and between wooden spoons

I am ashamed before the Great Tendency
to lean lamps against tables, for this
we forgive ourselves and are forgiven.

I am ashamed before the Great Liability
with which we clothe ourselves when we are
and when we are no more ourselves, say, in
garages.

I am ashamed before the Great Involvement
which never sleeps nor sees the line
between concrete and skin.

I am ashamed before the Great Concurrence
of the paper opening and closing its wings
of how we must hear our words before bows
fall.

I am ashamed before
the Great
Counteraction.

I am ashamed
before the Great Space
holy
holy
holy

I am ashamed before the Great Region of
where you
now are and am
he is the rose

I am ashamed before the Great Country.
He has set me in a broad place
penciled in with his kind hand.

I am ashamed before the Great Country of
the farthest fathering, and there am not
afraid.

I am ashamed before the Great City, O,
city of hymns and our tellings
of hymns in annums singing.

I am ashamed before the Great
location of mothers under the earth and in
the garage, pacing, reading clouds.

I am ashamed before the Great dislocation
of legs, tables out of order, awkward
collections of utensils in sinks.

I am ashamed before the Great
Presence of branches
skywriting.

I am ashamed before the Great Absence in
the bone of my bones
writing within me.

I am ashamed before the Great Habitation
humming and hearing and bowing before the
hymns begin.

I am ashamed before the Great Native
hibernation of snow in the clearing before
the first birth.

I am ashamed before the Great
inhabitation as if
you were running toward me in rain.

I am ashamed before the
Great Abode,
your pavilion is my crag.

I am ashamed before the Great
room with a door.

I am ashamed before the Container and
Contained with sense in its being, as a
high-flying plane reminds me of you.

I am ashamed before the Great Size
of one.

I am ashamed before the Greatness of each.

I am ashamed before the Great Expansion,
where is comfort but in the plane's stroke
over the back road.

I am ashamed before the Great Contraction:
something is slipping from above your
smile.

I am ashamed before the Great Distance
before my heart breaks for you in all
ways in the cloud of the spin.

I am ashamed before the nearness which
sees things which be not as though they
were.

I am ashamed before the Great
interval intact more than the
faces of things and the sound

I am ashamed before the Great Length of
light knotting itself in a cord for the
blind.

I am ashamed before you, Great shortness,
beneath the bed or were you here just now
a child breathing.

I am ashamed before the Great Breadth of
green when we were children constructing
masses with wood.

I am ashamed before the great
Narrowness because the way of the seeming
is the way of is
in the eyes of the generals.

I am ashamed before the Great Filament
of if spread within me
with the everlasting arm.

I am ashamed before the Great
Height of holy
turns, and the holding of this height.

I am ashamed before the Great
low wall beyond the sound of our harps,
which hears the harps and weeps.

I am ashamed before the Great Depth before
the Great grave of our fathers.

I am ashamed before the Great shallowness
of our memory and love
of our arms and deserts.

I am ashamed before the Great Top turning
west from the flesh toward Zion and north
from the lines between concrete and skin.

I am ashamed before the
Great bottomless blessing the
right and left closed me behind and before

I am ashamed before the Great vertical
brethren, I am wildly twisting in your
crosswalk over all bridges.

I am ashamed before the
horizontal beneath the
word and the
hands that turned it sideways.

I am ashamed before the great pendancy and
the wire the bird the wire the sky writing

I am ashamed before the Great support in
semblance, what we gather in our arms like
wheat.

I am ashamed before the Great Shaft
the knowing of the shaft, and the knowing
of the harvest because we are already
here.

I am ashamed before the
Great Parallel of crossed
love letters

I am ashamed before
the Great oblique
of a cool palm in the mind.

I am ashamed before the Great Inversion of
lost stones finding the farthest
spheres of geodes.

I am ashamed before the Great
crossing:
behind, above, before, below.

I am ashamed before the Great, great
weave
around the father.

I am ashamed before the Great Sewing
Machine
mother.

I am ashamed before the Great
exterior face we restitch,
because the plane leaves shortly.

I am ashamed before the Great interior
kitchen where the father's
wings open and close and newspapers
stack themselves by doors.

I am ashamed before the Great central
from which we must depart
because we love the father.

I am ashamed because the Great layer of
light is removing itself I am blind

and ashamed before the Great, Great
covering of priests
and hide my face on my knees.

I am ashamed before the Great
skin for which I am afraid. The house
warms. I step on flies.

I am ashamed before the Great Father in
all directions and of itself, before the
writing was read off the wall, before it fell from the peignoir.

I am ashamed before the great clothing we
have mended and forgiven, as we take it off and nail
ourselves to the way of the
river.

I am ashamed before the Great divestment.

I am ashamed
before the Great environs of fellows
waiting by wells.

I am the circumspection and the
light at the end of the hill
hosanna in peels by the side
of the road.

I am the bounds, the great enclosure
laughing lightly
because.

I am the interposition, the need to follow
the many rules, gladly—
short turnings toward the greater face.

I am contraposition, heavenward: I
remember:
on the road to St. Peter's.

I am the great front setting,
toward Jerusalem, toward Sumer, toward the
way toward, ho-ho—

I am the rear. I am the shadow yielding
there, in the cleft of the rock, the bosom
being with the need for being in the cleft

I am the side as seem, and then as the
seam, the small, barbaric knowledge of the
sewn, because our clothes must be torn,
and torn, and even then torn.

I am the right side swerve

I am the left side swerve

I am the structure already mended, here.
Such distant suns to have and hold.
Such remarkable adorations: we have been
redeemed.

I am the form of this earth I am the
formlessness carried along, an orange in
the pocket, chapter and verse, peeling
many suns as the   dogs   laugh
                                   with   me

I am the symmetry and

distortion
is this a ball in a box is this a face
looking back am I hanging by my wrists are
there ten apples is this number is this

I am the straightness of time when the
hand stills, when we hear the
stars

I am the the, angular step toward our
father, and
when we take leave toward the father.

I am the curve still coming, and now is—
its yoke lifts my head.
And now is

I am the circle under all cities and
within the avenues of cities and yet I am
the circle of the sea opening

I am the convolution of bridges and
circles of bridges, avenue of avenue, blue
milk spilling.

I am sphericity! Shall I tell you about
the leg shall I tell her I saw it grow
shall I say it was only two inches on the

tile, convexity. Two hands on the table,
wing tips,
cows, wine skins bursting new wine.

I am the sharpness of becoming,
nails scattered here and there,
ready for wood.

I am the blunt.
And even this, and this—
falling to fire.

I am the Great smooth curve, the I am
leg
the I am that I am.

I am the old rough coming back, to thee.
It is a long way and the wise never tire
and yet

I am the notch coming and going,
across old orders, erasing new as
if

I am the furrow in love: be this April
unmooring us, the one note on the back of
a birch bark.

I am your fold, the sheep of your pasture.
So gladly found
in the door between.

I am the opening.
As if a door is the only means of passing
from the kitchen to the garage.

I am the closed as if.
Before the leg there were rules.

I am the great motion of moments older
than.
and I am the falling up   to space

I am the quiescence of words taking shapes
on the floor as I walk over waves from the
kitchen to kitchens.

I am the swiftness subsiding as ashes
burn. I am the chariot of red hearts.
I am the still, swift wind above the
mound—

I am the great transference of shame and
the forgiveness of shame
having surfaces.

I am the great vehicle, tricycles
stationed around the father and the great
red and green wheels of his seed.

I am the one traveler, the white smear like
a dash and a dot,
the shoe, the shin, the high flying plane

I am the great traveler: for this I am
afraid, and dash back to the mother's
face.

I am the great water
traveler, the bird of paradise.

I am the great mariner's fish becomes bird
becomes face
becoming bird becoming fish becoming face:

I am the great boat
in which
he rose.

I am the great aviation in all ways, the
face in which you choose to walk, the
wider river of your stroke.

I am the Great Aircraft, soloing, high,
highest, lighting the dark from within the
dark as the door opens

I am the missilery. Forgive
us our trespasses as we forgive those who
trespass   within us.

I am the space traveling in three paths,
one paper on top one underneath one
between beyond and before:
you lay your palms out in this and we are
glad.

Here, I am the great impulse. Here.

I am the great reaction of bodies and
birds
lifting.

I am the great push of excessive
brightness driving me to the high
mount of the highest sun of the highest

I am the great pull of great-grandfathers'
names in ashes
for this we must be ashamed.

I am the leverage of your small tables,
your small hands on tables, and white
tablecloths.

I am the attraction of the whole. We are
not breaking the barriers, no.
We have been called holy and we must be.

I am the repulsion of war.
I am the not-turning
I am.

The air smells like a cage.
The air is the color of old lions.
The early light is exhausted.
I should be writing in sand.
My hand is chasing the edge.
I am too wild for shoes I am an old woman.
Things became after the leg.
A pant a shin a wingtip.
The buzz of lamps the angels singing they
were singing. Yes.

I am the direction, here.

I am the great deviation away
from war.
This is not about miracles this is not
about the way things can be this is about
the way things are the way things are in
the world.

I am the leading of sand, forgiven deserts
I am the palms' flight in winter when it's
hot I am the monarch of the pilot dreaming

I am the following day remaining the same.
I am the yes of the flight and the no of
the same flight.

I am the great progression home to all old
garages, fathers, sisters, brothers, great
garages in mansions, hospitals, hospitals.

I am   the regression   after the
generals go home: in this the
mind divides.

I am the approach beyond approach. I am
the end of the general stylus.

I am receding the years of your deserts—I
am the cleft of pavilions the color of
sand.

I am the converging "let there be"

always already diverging toward here.

I am arrival hearing all barriers
and loving them as it breaks.

I am vast departures of pastures, vastly
from my vast having-departed, and of
these I weep.

I am your entrance, flickering and
slovenly, big bosomed, bearded.

I am the emergence of color the concrete
of skin and the inability of water to
support a man walking.

I am the great insertion of the last men
of the last days in the last and bloody
battles: for this we must be afraid.

I am the great extraction;
breath breathing breathed.

I am   the   alpha's reception
of omega's constellation.

I am the great extraction of death in grass: I
cannot live in amazement.

I am emergence: the road of potential is
the way of madness.

I am the entrance of all soloists
because outside, in fact, there remained.

I am the first ejection (the trees are in
the right places) at all-times-X
the secret place of the Most High.

Forgive us our shortcomings in time.
Forgive us our decisions through glass.
Looking back, we see you as we have seen.

The ascent infinitely folds itself back,
again, with broad, broad love   a thousand
and ten angels singing they were singing
Yes.

The descent of garages and the ascent   up
the stairs to the second floors where   we
heard the mother's calls before the mother
of elevation speaks:

You are a bell writing of madness.
You are the rose and the cup of water.
You rose between water in moments.

Circumstances over-fenced
around the straight edges by bushes and shrubs
collapsing rotation

always in isolation
ovens remain clean,
mushrooms balance over cities,
coffee rumbles over deserts.

You are the agitation of memory
the humming refrigerator clock expanding
at the back of the stove as if air
conditioning were blowing through vents

as the physics of midsummer
Sundays when grass dies.

He is sitting at tables
smelling like showers.

He is the darkness on pages at
all times, all pages once, twice
y-words and winds catching my iris.

He is
the heat of cedars on stoves: do not take
time passing (at the back of stoves)
for the velocity of apples.

You are the sea's cook of orange Africas.
You are the fuel not subject to gravity, names,
wars as choices

we tend not to make,
incombustibles walking the straight edge of waves.

This is the effort: our cold warms us.
We are reflected in blades and not palms
of spoons: we do not see ourselves in
deserts or as drawers open: she opens
the drawer and curves into herself,

saying as, as refrigeration:

the laws of cause and effect are true. Say you become
light with grace. We have learned how to stack newspapers
and build for we look not at things which are seen.
I am the light source of wells above rivers, the ashcat's
grin, the one fin above the bosom-fish,

a shade above transparence: this is about how the oven
door reflected light, how a third mouth sings
semitransparencies: this the river I felt as a child.

Opaque strings wound my branches and played, fields of
strings tuning white electric blue from all sides.

My electronics of mid-being, delusions of sitting at
tables, having hands, driving in cars, cows kneeling.

Opaque: things were heavy with rocks and my mouth is
jeweled semitransparent with traces of transparent green
stones above stones beneath rocks in pockets.

You are the mechanics of the
mind's involvement.

You are the tool, a black coal,
here.

Independent automation tears my branch, my line between
glass and wood,

frictions even here, marks and move-
ments of this singular list of a last list. Textures.

Old density, you, on the walk over waves, in the tree of
the road and the dream of the road.

Beside all rarity, beside the between and the passing of
yellow trucks

rigidities race horses:
this is the most difficult
leaving of wind, in stems

and roots, in such new
pliancies, say, stepping
on cracks.

The Great Elastic and to end,
resonating,

touching joy in trees,
clapping.

Oh, fragility, the world
settles in

you are the color as
and yet you are in front
flying

you are the color sitting on a mountain
I was circling overhead I was the
circle,

colorless, I was the as if
and the being of the yet
whiteness, I was and I was my being of the seem

blackness, the being of the yet and the

grayness, desire

brown, fine white knot, here

red (pale ends)
orange fins, sliced wave,
yellow,

green eyes and silver mouths,
blue inventions and inventions of a clearing.
Purpleness holding and the being held,

variegated gravings of the general,
universe of hymns in the small
square box on the shelf

ashes ashes materialities bones bones bones and a box of a
thousand pencils

immaterialities yellow-heavy
as fire tries to surface
as we choose to begin:

You are materials of mothers:
Husky pencils too fat for
such small hands.

You are the immaterial sleeping
in red chairs
(her hand on her chest, his blue suit)

You are the yes I saw written
in trees,

bones, bones, bones and a box
in a closet.

Inorganic matters for father,
lakes in space.
Above all our minerals, between

the palms and around the rock
of heaven and earth
You are the rock, movement of palms.

Pace before the call: I forgive you.
Body of land: I forgive you.

plain land of towns, hotels, kitchens, muddy letters,
hens scratching

I have enclosed you in image, willows
and cascading wells I have lost my color to you.

Knowledge of distinction, knowledge of final
participations, solutions, dry palms as he kneels and we
kneel

before the general effort,
before the open grace, pistol
placed

a late winter fly
on our neck.
It is raining, Mother.

Mother-streaming, gigantic
in hours, were old patterns
of beds and systems of

roots such unholy channels?
For this we soil our hands.
For this we remain beige.

Ocean wingtips, my providers,
your grace is sufficiently
pinioned.

Bone, lake, wind,
inlet pencils.

Small stones in the kitchen marsh,
pages through yellow pages.
Now is not the time for the dash.
Now is not the time for correct imagery.

Be thou the air I breathe just now.
Be thou the second bird behind the first
and the silence behind the rest.

My hands in wind lettering-go.
Flights.
Clouds in the kitchen. I am trying to walk plainly,
unappeased by clouds.

Wind, newspapers, organic matters from the stairhead. He
was the good
father and is—

you are the life, flesh
spoken out of existence.
You are not the death

we continue to be with each
turn toward garages.
You are not killing, the

landing-places of flight.
You are more than the rivers' harbor.
More than such boxes on shelves, on far peripheries.

More than the front time dividing the rest.
We mutter along grounds in figures,
we forgive ourselves death.

Violent paginations still
drawn between skin and cement
and green marble.

We must not stop in cars
as we don't know where
to begin when the road is present.

We must seek the speed
of peripheries in death,
forgetting our names.

We must call this
awaking-is-to-call-back
toward sleep.

We must, in the beginning.
The leg is growing toward itself.
Issac to the mount, again.

We will be silent.
We will be silent.
We will be silent.

We stop the gaze—
the footprints of the first step
land before we fall.

Yeshua of flocks,
holy beginning and never-ending above

Vision hunting as we look back, here,
into the kingdom, here,
lion of lions of Judah.

It is you and you and that
man over there and this
girl at the next table

We miss the mother's face,
the sensation of the whole
tenderness and tables,

an elsewhere in ourselves for holy readings, silk pages in
drawers. Think of roses—
water in a glass
before bed

With an eye in the blue
not the mind of thee
looking-at

green walls. Our
garden she keeps
in mind

Touching us like triplets
of the day below
windows

Surface-swimming the surface
with Great
faces of kings

You are the great chain of sun-words
we speak
spirit and lose ourselves

Imaginations cease before
thrones. And even this
will cease though I speak with angels

our high love must,
to ready the higher
as we ready cool cloths

One for beauty
One for wings
One for Yeshua, Adonai
Adonai

Rafts to your poolsides
Yellow, blue
playing here

You have made your acts
to be remembered
as you remember us
as we keep renewing

Trust in fountains
above the road rising
out of breath toward vision.

At the edge of the mind
a light fountain splashing

toward perceptions of
fragrance of
valerianaheel.

We are blind for you, heart swimming.
Our glass filled
and is filling,

Great spectator dreaming
of seeing my
gaze, I am

the apple of eyes
visible breathing
in light:

sweet, sweet
visible
invincible

disappearance
let me rise by the front fender

hearing the way
of all beginnings
deaf to the lettering-go

the great sound stream
silence our mother
faintness of sound dear father

loudness there is our hand
resonance here is our palm
repeated sounds there our harbors

explosive noise our Word
sibilation of sun
stridor our third twin you love

call the of-is an is
palms matching exactly
Elysium of your kitchen of mansions

instruments wildly laughing
palms roots stems wind
bones bones

wisdom wildly twisting
wise women in embers
foolish scripts erasing

these fields these lips
in clouds fool
the lions are alive

in the air again
more than momentarily
lions in stems and

in roots and in the
difference between
one word and the next

more than cows in fields
more than an occasion of
memory slanting

through doors more
than curling leaves
between blades along

systems from willows to
houses up walls through
windows to mirrors

to beds and loving
cups: I am
idea as forgiveness

absence of thought
the poem the occasion
opening west the

walls are a womb
the harbor of rivers
a well the harbor

as rivers in wells
I am kneeling
his harbor his chest
Adonai-breathing
-seeding
bones

father-dying
-calling
wings

the call from the stair
the forgiveness of miracles
the forgiveness of garages

I am the yes

judgment: I am the yes
kitchen garages seeding machines
forgive me

beds tables stairs spoons
forgive me
blood stones stems

forgive me
lion hawk
forgive me

father mother
father mother
father mother

I bow before the great music playing after
us as color catching up with its orchid as
it turns within the heart of still fathers

I worship the Great Harmonic, the one note
of future-forgetting.

I worship the Great Instrument.
Here, we find him there,
forever hearing.

I worship the Great Becoming-after-Mind
soon lost
and turn from signs toward
orchestras, weeping.

I worship the Great Weeping-for-wise-men,
poor fools, we lay our palms out, we weep
for the love of We-lay-our-palms-out, no-
mind.

I worship the Holy Unintelligence beyond
the Holy Sign for Intelligence and the
holy.

I worship the Great
Foolishness moving
my colors toward plum orchids.

I worship the Great labor of the Fool
who has no name beside the fool.

I worship our vast sanity, let this
holy spirit be,
Holy Spirit, Be.

I worship the arrow of the insane
blindness walking over waves
between the kitchen and garage.

I worship the most golden eccentricity.
Geese in reverse, cows kneeling,
sunset like a skid.

I worship the great comprehension of fact.
There, on the table, spoons, forks, salt,
pepper, arranged in a line Mary Visits
Every Sunday.

I worship You, Great Knowledge. So much
to love, our hearts on earth, our hearths'
hearing.

I worship this great Ignorance, holy
no-mind. The yes and yes and yet:
Great, great fathers humming for us.

I worship the Great Thought of no-Thought
as it settles like risen toast, as we rise
in the morning.

I worship the Great Absence of no-thought,
thoroughly here in no-time,
even before the short dash.

I worship the vast Intuition, spreading
its palms out,
green meaning-to breaths.

I worship the sweet reasoning.
The great taking-toward the old
apple core below the desk.

I am afraid to worship the great
Consideration. Because my lamp is so
dull, because I have forgotten to light it

I worship the Great grace of inquiry, the
palm waving us through the door,
gracefully, gracefully.

I worship the Great Answer, because I
must. I consider desert wings, I consider
the tip of the flown wing, I consider the
graceful wing.

I worship the Beyond of small solutions,
because of the yin-yang of peasant shoes
and the written speech of fools written in

Because our love for you is the Great
discovery, greater even than this love,
or the small solutions of love, —

Because we want the Great Experiment to be
true.
Yes, this, last night, I.

Because we want the Great Measurement of
words with worlds and not at all

We worship the Great Holy Discrimination.
We take our vows solemnly.
We forget our vows most thankfully.

I worship the Great Indiscrimination Yes.
I am a slave to your love this fair bright
crossing.

I worship the
Great, magnificent Judgment of Yes written
between stars, —.

I worship the slow Prejudgment wiping the
sky clean.
May we hold your ring finger and wait,—

I worship the Great Misjudgment
in love
despite itself.

I worship the Great Estimations we keep on
shelves, figuring
so many pencils in such a vast box.

I worship the ordinary Supposition of this
ancient gathering of will
pushing ourselves over lines.

I worship the Not-Philosophy breathing
just.
Such broad love, oh holy.

I worship the Great Belief handed down,
in pods, in smaller keys than doors for
the largest heart, in which we hide our
face, oh holy, our many faces, oh holy.

I worship the Great Credulity laughing.
Golden leaves as lips, butterhands, dainty
veins in wings, liquid architectures,
rain.

I worship the Great Unbelief we run after,
retracing our steps as if for the next
time-as we promise, again.

I worship the last ground for belief, the
straightforward's way-in garage,
irrevocable jars, minutes in burlap.

I worship the Great Evidence of rules,
rain, flat figurations
and walk behind them as kings and queens

because I am ashamed and worship the
Great Qualification
to lose my sense of color.

Because the Great No-Qualification,
because of this and no-more,
pine needles, past and present
declensions,

I worship such small possibilities and am,
on the way-toward-in
returning.

I worship the hand holding impossibility
letting itself go in my soul, and beneath
my loss of soul.

I worship the Great, savage probability.
Lion of Judah, thousand eyes of the woods
where we were children.

I worship the Great singular
improbability—we must choose to turn even
from this and this, and beyond this, love.

I worship the need for the Great Certainty, as
a wake flawlessly passing,
mighty redundancies.

Holy. I worship the uncertain, and mourn
myself gladly
and am found.

Holy. I worship the Great Conformity
to fact which pardons
the line between skin and skin.

Because of this great truth, I forgive
this night. Because of this great truth,
I forgive this day. Because of this great
truth, I-this.

I worship the holy Maxim expanding.
Martha Martha Martha Martha Martha.
Mary Mary Mary Mary Mary Mary Mary.

I worship the just Error, un-traced.
The hem, the shoe:
so be it by appearance.

I worship the holy one illusion longing
for company, becausing the great human.
Yeshua, Adonai, Adonai, Adonai.

I worship such acceptance as we have,
bread without sugar,
kind fathers reminding us of someone.

I worship the infinite Assent
on streetcorners, in beige coats, books in
hand.

I worship this fine Dissent,
filaments as if,
later geometries.

I worship the Affirmation
late winter
branches

Great Negations Great Denials
wedding containers containing
the wet voice of St. Peter's.

I worship the great slovenly mind,
reliquary,
bones bones bones and a box.

I worship the holy broadness back to the
page: hieroglyphs pinned down, the little
demands of a day, flowers, riding buses,

as if such narrowness to be

because we write small curiosities.
Because it's hard to remember the rule for
the day: flowers, ride buses, walk
plainly,

I worship the High Incuriosity.
The hawk in the shape of a mountain.
Here I am, this-is-where I am.

I worship the Great
Attention forgotten-not-made.

I worship the bowed inattention
of tables
(whose gravity offers forgiveness).

I worship the stretched distraction
healing between the bed of the
mind and the body's bed.

I worship the Great carefulness coming
toward the peripheries' mad velocities.

I worship the Great Neglect at the door,
leaving the knob on the sill,
walking on the edge of dark carpets.

I worship the Great Imagination Rocking.
We sing to ourselves and the planets sing
to ourselves.

I worship the Great Recollection folding
lawnchairs, getting off the
bus to remember rain

I worship the Great Memory
calling upon evening to listen to bones
bones bones bones bones bones bones bones.

I worship the Great Shape
of our forgetfulness
within me.

I worship the Seen of Anticipation
reaching lines before the reaching-toward

before-the-Great Expectation.
So many branches to love writing
themselves on our faces.

We bow before the inexpectation
of the war at hand
erasing us before ourselves.

We worship the constant Prediction
turning beside itself
neither-falling neither-rising
always-falling-always rising

I mourn for the Presentiment of music
returning me to earth
to remember my name.

I mourn for the nature of ideas
communicated.
Your sad eyes know nothing of the none.

I mourn for this meaning-beyond-music,
dissonance that-away:
because we forget the old bone masks
beneath.

I mourn for the great Thee-
Meaninglessness. As,
record needles
erasing light.

I mourn for the Great Intelligibility.
The reunion of soon
with alto saxes.

I mourn for this two-tone
Unintelligibility.
I am afraid for the books of jazz.
I am afraid for heralds.

I mourn before walls of interpretation.
Because we made masks for days,
because we will know him when he's gone.

I mourn before the old ambiguities,
between worlds words fall,
between words we fall,
between falls we fall,
Peter, my flying.

I mourn again, before these figures
speaking as I hear
as I am hearing.

I mourn for this, that we are so lost
in our manifestations of phantoms, how we
want to be loved to want to be loved to
be.

I mourn before this great disclosure, this
day, from the marrow of the bone
he paints rainbows on.

I mourn before the information
opens and we see as he must see: just as,
he leaves,
he wants to remind us.

I mourn before the news arrives
as he leans into silence
for us.

I mourn before the known communication and
say yes,
and gladly, yes.

I mourn before the great messenger plain
writing in sand and far from sand in great
strokes on a great gray ashcat.

We bow before the morning of will, when he
departs from himself, sliding up the sun's
ladder, with a hoo-ha, with a hoo-hoo-hoo.

I mourn the great loss of willingness
to paint masks in the morning and say
somebody maybe somebody maybe somebody
maybe

In this infinite unwillingness
we wait as ice
on ice floes

I mourn before the great misteaching,
and correct myself: he is not the hum
before the fall he is our one note, here.

I mourn instead, learning how to wrap
rocks in paper and paint them,
this one red this one orange this one
yellow this one green this one blue this
one pink we mix, this violet, whose roots
will rise.

I mourn for the way we enter these
Teachers. And I mourn for the way we
enter these forget-to-enter-these-
Teachers.

I mourn for the leaving-to students,
forgetting Copernicus,
and forgetting also.

I mourn for the vast-school-as
and erase
the grave to have ears to hear.

I mourn for the road's indications,
circles of squares of
insignias of last resignations

imperfectly drawn with pencils.
Because the return is so far,
we lay our book down, and begin to read:

As-every-every, time.
As-every-ever, place.
We mourn here for the record
of future astonishment.

I run after the great representation.
Because we long to repeat days.
Because we find ourselves in the middle of
the wrong street—

we run for the covers of
misrepresentation, as,
if, here, then, you, the highest candle
like, a sea-gram opening,

as-if to forgive us our language
when parents drive off
and the endgames begin

without the truth of letters, just the
affect of an African style and
mystical muddles—

This. I am ashamed. Before becoming
blind, I see the
before-becoming Word.

Before becoming deaf, I hear the
Nomenclature clapping in the one clap hall
as the bombs drop and Issac continues to
play.

Before becoming mute, I speak with
Anonymity, and hear myself even as
I-am heard: ma ma mai ma ma ma ma

Before-becoming lame, I walk with an old
woman limping, collecting cans
and jars, leaving three tracks.

I bow above becoming-grammar, as
an angel on the waves between
the kitchen and garage.

Style my Angel came
walking with bare feet,
collecting shells.

Elegance my Angel came running,
again I say rejoice!
Rejoice rejoice again I say rejoice!

inelegant angel of rivers
flow toward me/
as-ice in summer/

Plain Speech my Angel calls
every third wave

and now I know conciseness is lost
and now I know diffuseness is lost

I mourn before the spoken language.
Because we lose the tick-tock and the time
still-moves,

between the bottom of the bag and the
earth and itself, we seek speech, and do
not find it there.

Between the imperfect speech and the earth
and itself, we seek peace, and do
not find it there.

Between the talk and the constricting
invisible, we seek perfection, and do
not find it.

Between conversations, we seek revelations
about near folding far about near, old
hens nesting.

—I detach myself from soliloquies

—as

—a weather vane

I am within the lamb of El

as

in Elegance,

I am the Great Grandiloquence speaking, as
geese, as lettering-knots in the nightsky,

I am the hearing written languages,
self-persuasions overhead,
something about the being-in-between—

I am the Great Writing Back,
loveletter,

the Great Print,
seen with such large letters,
I write with a large voice,

I am your Great Correspondence—to tell is
to disbelieve madness, to believe in legs
growing, to see buses driving toward
presence O

Holy Book, stationery of the one cross,
Holy Book, dialects of the twiced love,
Holy Book, breath, breathing, breathed,

I am your Great Treatise, to speak
is to misspell gladness as
flocks of geese,

Holy Book, abridgment of the one cross,
Holy Book, description of your
third love,

I am your poem on the sill, just
blown off and carried
away by wind, here,

Hosanna, Great Prose, basket of wheat
filling our staffs with your sky blue,
I am your entertainer, sky blue,

space of small secrecies
between ourselves, acts, and habits,
the mountain and garage,

and I am ashamed between
such light concealments
in the wisdom of imagining,

I am ashamed of this falsehood:
I have seen the leg of consumptions and
tending,

I am ashamed of this exaggeration:
how do I work and live when the world is
crowned so,

I am ashamed of this deception:
within the imagination, the gray dress of
the garage,

this deceiver: boxes fall and fold and
trash cans cinch themselves

with empty incantations, stack their
words in temples made with multiple
perspectives.

Selah.
Selah.
Selah.

I come to bring the seemings to the seen,
to stain the summer wild for the severing
of so many springs, so many   springs.

And from this harmonious soon, I turn.
Because in that day
he assembles the lame

to turn toward this turn with willingness
gathering outcasts

because the unison of stars turns
twice, as we are twiced, and twice loved,
because of our kindly unwillingness,

because our father prunes such high notes
from the willow and the palm,
we turn from this resolution together.

Because the words once lined up for duty,
and we used them in love songs, for
mowing lawns, we choose to love them, to
persevere.

I am ashamed before irresolution, the
great faux-between
root.

I am ashamed before the change of
allegiance April flowers
in the wrong garden.

I am ashamed before the all-impulsive,
my weather vane, my rock.

I am ashamed before the great evasion
as we turn the other cheek toward those
coming toward us.

I am ashamed before the great avoidance,
and this too is forgiven, this time with
candor.

I am ashamed before the great
escape toward you, and laugh great red
roses.

I am ashamed before the
abandonment, when we wrapped our minds around trees.

I am ashamed before the inclination to
climb them, before the need for the fall
from the fig tree's not-knowing-again.

I am shame before the blessing of desire,
the one note we hear only
on the bias.

The eagerness of lost souls beneath the
merry mound, a kind of purgatorio mime.

Maker of most holy indifference, forgive
us. Maker of forgetfulness,
forgive us our tragic minds.

We are erasing our most holy choices, now.
We are returning to known, now.
Forgive us, father.

Such sad rejections:
all the fish thrown back,
the fertilizer scattered.

Such small necessities:
pencils, a box, a bed, gardens.

Such far predeterminations:
that man at this last table,
perspectives from above and below
rather too familiar.

Such old prearrangements:
at every moment we choose
this and this and this

and we begin to speak customs,
such as plain schedules:
Mary visits every Sunday.

And time seems to open fashionably.
But we go back, to the edge of the corner
because of the excessive turn,

and remember the willow, and remember the
many formalities mother taught us:
do not lie do not lie do not lie do not lie

Cars stand still, informally. We neither
sow nor reap and   yet
and   yet:

we laugh at ourselves in a time of war.
We are ashamed before the great
motivation.

We are ashamed above the distant pretext:
each false line begins here   lie do not
lie.

Such small, grave allurements.
We teeter-totter and dwell.
We strap ourselves to the ship,

small bribes.
Forgive us our infinite excuse to be
loved.

How far toward dissuasion we remain,
the war at hand never winning as it crawls
along the bottom of the sea,

head back to drink the last drop.
How far this original purpose comes
to join us this evening.

One-legged, then two, miracles, miracles,
excessive intention driving us forward, too
impatient to wait.

Back to the main idea, the plan prehanded.
Back to the pursuit of heavenly bodies.
Back to the all there is.

Back to business as usual,
the father's occupation:
prune willows, keep the grass very green.

Back again to the ways and means here:
first, we lose the arms, then we share
this skin, then we say holy, emptiness

I am ashamed before the great provision.
Beneath our yard efforts, we flower
like buried boards.

Before the great supply, we demand
that we be loved,
strapped onto our own buckets.

And before this, we turn back to the all-
sufficient one.

And before this, to the insufficient
response
spinning in our palms.

To the every-excess cone
inside the contemplation
of the spin.

To every-use spilling over.
To the half-consumed explosion.
To the half-misuse folded back.
To the known forgiven—

We turn back to the small fields before
now and remark their uselessness, and
worship you there.

And for this, we turn to the dead,
my fathers about me
my mothers about me
and remark their adaptation to ends.

From now on we hear them singing:
wholesomeness, and mourn with them
because we lost our soul,

your initial in my ashes,
your names in their smoke:
this is the cross

O holy Name,
O Holy Silence Beyond Names
O Holy.

We have lost our health, here.
We prefer the seeming promise of an always
already ineffable to tedious, successful
explanations.

We have lost our emptiness with sight,
O, holy coming back.
We turn from physical progress.

We have lost this security,
the memory of concepts upon which my
father lifts me.

We have lost the Voluntary Action,
Christ have mercy.
And from this, love, we turn, even,
from the absence of the mind's narrow.

We have lost the Endeavor, mother. Keep
my eyes on your constant arriving, on the
shelves, here.

I see your names there, in my father's
fathers' names,
the preparation of the call down-sight of
mutual vastness.

I see your name in the accomplishment of
the call be ye:
we cannot help ourselves in this missing
topic, origin-X.

We see your name adroit, relatively,
because we loved our negations as our aim,
because we cast ourselves off

and see your name in broad love of holy
kitchen conduct: and now forgive
ourselves for this immense forgetting,

in the more difficult pitch, we hear our
prerogative, and then the heart
forgetting, and then the turning away from
the turning—

I am ashamed before the Great Government
in hundreds of skies neither Northern nor
fiery but just a white night with a few
infinite stars.

We seek the infinite direction, here,
and remain ashamed,
being the last miracle on the bus.

We seek the finite directions between
the great shame of discovery
and the garage

because the going back is so far,
because the effort is the loss-of,
because of this, we cannot go back,

or must go with restraint, with things,
because the streets are always already
constructed, because compliance with the
map is wrong,

because we pledge this: this is not about
miracles this is not imperfect to the way
things can be on a single surface,

this has passed through many hands,
being none other than consent.
And from this ground, we turn

from the dead—
Danaides, Ixions, Sisyphus—
and ask their forgiveness.

At the end of mind, words soften in peace.
At the end of your world the words turn,
and we are seen as we have seen our
sights.

This is the holy possession of paths:
invisible ink, lofty lover, big breeze,
wild flowers.

This is the sharing of paths,
so many sounds, so many sounds.

And this is the appropriation:
and now I go back to the ashes, the small
starts I made above now, such sorry
palimpsests you are

And now I go back to the holy emotion,
to the faces of fathers, turned
toward my door, waiting for my arrival how
long you've waited.

And now I go back to the most holy
excitability:
I've only now heard your names
in my names for you.

I've only now seen my names in my names
for you, late fathers of a latter
daughter.

And now I go back to the holy pleasure and
pleasureableness.
As a tree lets its leaves fall, this line
comes back to Dublin, the way of flesh
now with mercy.

As now to the holy anticipative emotion:
for the just there is no law,
for the traveler, no street that is not
known.

And now to the glory of concern,
great bosom becoming.

And now I go back to discriminative
affections, this is
the pianist humming
this is the conductor humming
this is the orchestra humming with itself,
to itself, because of the love
that moves the strings
and the bows across the string,
before they know of the being-bowed.

Forgive us our pride
where there is nothing nothing
and even on the Mount nothing, toward
widening.

Forgive us our esteem.
To be the not-knowing is to come by the
way beyond.

Forgive us our being-beyond contemplative
emotions:
.   wonder
unastonishment
wonder
unastonishment

For we have lost the social relations.
We lose speech. We hear the one note, not
the adagio, not the harmony that plays the
string back to refrigerators

and their pictures on refrigerator doors,
turned right and left, watching me coming
and going, such broad love, such broad
love O holy

For we have lost the social affections
and in this nakedness of spirit find rest

in which we bow to benevolence,
a lively andante.
How the conductor breathes, how we hear
his loss and move on, farther along our
mutual selves.

In which we bow to sympathy,
until one note sounds in the soul,
and all things are constant.

In which we bow to gratefulness,
and return to the shelves and the name of
the father, Old, old master.

And turn from ill humor
(You are so gladly found).

And turn from selfish resentment.
I will not delight in the names on books.
My tastes are so changed having read them.

We have forgotten the wings of morals
and the lightning of the lift: the end
of such days of increasing sunsets
and the end of that end.

We have forgotten the winds of moral
obligations, so holy, take me back to the
names speaking back,
before the hearing of the heard.

We have forgotten the holy moral sentiment
out of the arc out of the light and back,
such large arms to hold such a young traveler.

I double-back to the moral condition:
I've lost my footholds along the way,
thank you Father.
I've lost the center-sight of peripheries,
thank you Father.
I've lost the knowledge of you,
thank you.
And here, the mother's face, the notes
penned in a hurry.

I double-back to the moral practice:
saying everything, dashes, dots, something
about antifreeze, plain speech, plaid
couches, postcards for the wall.

I double-back to the moral observance.
Virgin down the road, weigh me to earth
weigh me to sky with itself sweet sister
yet

and yet, the saints take me back
to Dublin
where we meet an old, old street where we
have never been, still, yet, and again

and yet, in the heavens of music
we play with our humming

and yet, in sanctity
the way of the hand on the page
the way of a traveler down the road
the way of the eye lingers on the top shelf
forgetting your name

and yet, in worship
and now you are the one note flying
and now you are green
and now you are a car painting the street
red then green

and yet, in worship
a slight breath, a vibrato, the hand
stills

and yet, in worship
we wonder what others talk about as they
drive we wonder how they carry on
our conversations

and yet, in worship
we consider tender incidentals, anti-
freeze for the car
because of the mother's note

and yet, in worship
because of the rod that bent the cone
because of the cone that bent the child
because of the child unbending the world

because of the first cause of the last
breath

and yet
we mourn these apprehensions before we
step off

and yet, we seek
spontaneity because grandeur is slow
coming

and yet, we forgive
the farthest stars of pin-tips
our feathers on the wave-tips

and yet, we bow
in reflections

and yet, we worship
and speak quite figuratively

and yet
we forgive

and yet, in the great church
the stars are at the periphery
and we are gone